MW00878325

ELECTRONIC MUSIC: 25 MIXING TIPS FOR MODERN ELECTRONIC MUSIC PRODUCTION

ROY WILKENFELD

Copyright © 2015 Roy Wilkenfeld

All Rights Reserved.

This is a work of fiction. Names, characters, places, and incidents are a product of the author's imagination. Any resemblance to actual persons, events, or locales is entirely coincidental.

This book or any portion thereof may not be reproduced or used in any manner whatsoever without the express written permission of the author except for the use of brief quotations in a book review.

The information provided in this book is meant to supplement, not replace, any proper training in the field of music.

All images used in this book are Royalty Free and/or fall under the Creative Commons license.

ISBN-13: 978-1519107503

ISBN-10: 1519107501

What Is This eBook?

Electronic Music: 25 Mixing Tips for Modern Electronic Music Production is a mixing handbook for electronic music producers, containing 25 hand-picked methods that are designed to improve electronic music and dance music mixes.

The book does not contain all there is to know about mixing, but includes important fundamentals that construct a tight electronic music mix all the way to some of the more advanced techniques that experienced producers and mixers use.

This book is divided into five sections: Mix Essentials, Mix Clarity, Drum Sweetening, Special Stereo Width and Advanced Mixing Techniques.

Mix Essentials and Mix Clarity offer a strong base for any mix, with fundamental techniques that are important to get right for a clear and tight mix.

Drum Sweetening is a section for processing the most important parts of any electronic and dance track, the drums.

Mixes are getting wider in terms of the stereo field, and the Special Stereo Width -section offers some tricks for achieving that extra spice in terms of width.

Last but not least, the Advanced Mixing Techniques -section explains some of the more advanced but essential mixing methods for making a professional sounding track.

How to Use This Book

There are several ways to use this book. Think of it as a technical and creative handbook for mixing and producing electronic music.

One method is to read it through once while learning, and come back to the points you need help with during your mixes and production.

Another method is to use the table of contents as a guide to mixing. You will easily find the solution for your problem at hand in there.

You are encouraged to take the tips offered in this book to the next level, only limited by your own creativity. Think of the tips as guides to where you want your music and mixing to eventually go towards. After all, everyone mixes in their own unique way.

It is recommended you have this book available close by when you start mixing or producing for best effect, so the creative flow is not interrupted.

CONTENTS

INTRODUCTION

Mixing is a creative process that spans over different fields of focus. In this book, you will learn about the essentials of mixing, clarifying a mix, processing your drum samples, creating stereo width and advanced mixing techniques that could give your mixes that polished, professional touch.

This book includes 25 mixing tips on five different areas of mixing, with descriptions and tutorials to get you going in your mix. The book starts with mixing fundamentals and foundations and moves on to more advanced techniques.

You'll get straight into the mixing action by reading this book.

Have fun with mixing and learning!

-Roy Wilkenfeld

CHAPTER 1 MIX ESSENTIALS

01 GAIN STAGING

The purpose of gain staging is to set a healthy volume level for each instrument or audio signal before they reach the mixer fader.

Gain staging means that if a mixer channel fader was set to 0dB (a.k.a. *unity*), the signal going through that channel would peak somewhere between -6 to -20dBFS on the digital meter. Gain staging is the first thing to do in a mix. It is also one of the most important steps in mixing to ensure a clean, dynamic mix with lots of headroom in the master fader. When every single mixer channel is gain staged properly, they will form a healthy stereo mix, meaning the master track. Gain staging properly results in a healthy dynamic range and a great starting point for any mix. Gain staging inside a DAW can be done with any plugin able to control volume, such as the free Sonalksis FreeG, or any other trim plugin.

How to: Gain Stage a Mix

1. Insert a trim plugin on every mix channel.

2. Solo the first mix channel or mute all other channels.

3. Adjust the gain from the plugin for the first channel to peak between -6 and -20dbFS.

4. Repeat the procedure for the rest of the mixer channels.

Pro Tip #1: Set all mixer faders to unity and create a mix using only gain staging. Afterwards, you can fine-tune the mix with the mixer faders, taking advantage of the enhanced fader resolution. Mixer faders are not linear in volume, and have a greater resolution near 0dB.

Pro Tip #2: Don't stress about the exact level of a signal. As a rule of thumb, just make sure to keep your signals well below the 0dB line on your mixer channels.

Chapter 1 Mix Essentials

02 PANNING

Panning is used to spread sound sources in the stereo field.

In panning, sounds can be placed in the stereo field from far left and right to any position in between. One of the road-tested methods of panning is to use five different pan locations: far left (100%), left middle (50%), center (0%), right middle (50%) and far right (100%). By using this method, you will achieve a wide, lively mix by strategically panning instruments. Panning is done by using the circular pan knob located in a DAW's mixer channel. The advantages of panning are: it creates interest for the listener and even a simple song can be made interesting by the clever usage of panning. Panning is a mixing tool creating instrument separation and stereo width.

How to: Pan a drum kit (kick, clap, hi-hat, ride, wood percussion, congas)

1. Leave the kick and clap centered (0%).

2. Pan the hi-hat at left middle (50%) and the ride at right middle (50%).

3. Pan the wood percussion far left (100%) and congas and far right (100%).

4. The drums are now separated resulting in air and stereo width.

Pro Tip #1: Pan mono sources for best effect, because the location of a mono audio source can be pinpointed with panning.

Pro Tip #2: As a rule of thumb, keep the most important elements in a mix centered, such as the kick drum, snare, vocal and sub bass. Remember, there are no absolute rules in panning as in the end it is a matter of taste. Some like to pan different instruments differently. Take note of the method taught above and experiment with it.

Chapter 1 Mix Essentials

03 MIXER FADER BALANCE

90% of any mix is achieved by a correct balance using the mixer faders alone, hence the word "mixing".

The faders are the most important tool in mixing, hands down. Only 10% of a mix is done using EQ, compression and effects, merely polishing and stylizing a mix. For this reason, the mixer fader cannot be underestimated, as it ultimately is the mixer's best friend. Every DAW has its own mixer but the faders work almost identically from DAW to DAW.

How to: Create a good fader mix

1. After properly gain staging your mix, pull all mixer faders to silence (down completely).

2. Bring up the most important element, such as the kick drum. You should be able to bring the fader to the unity position if you have gain staged correctly.

3. Start bringing up the second important element, such as bass, lead or a vocal. Adjust the fader until it starts to "sit" with the most important element.

4. Take the next element in order of importance and bring it up, again adjusting and adapting to the on-going mix.

5. If needed, fine tune the fader positions of the already audible elements in the mix to tighten and glue the mix.

6. Repeat steps 4 and 5.

Pro Tip #1: By systematically mixing the most important elements of a song first, they will dominate the mix because the more elements you bring into a mix the more you will have to work to find space for them. This way, the less important elements do not get in the way of the more important ones.

Pro Tip #2: Create instrument groups, so all drums, basses, music and vocals can be controlled by their own single faders. By creating these groups (also known as buses or auxes) the mixer is able to fine-tune the relative levels of whole instrument groups at once, making level balancing a joy to do.

Pro Tip #3: Think of mixing like building a house, brick by brick. You'll need to insert each one to its place carefully.

04 MIX VOLUME LEVELS AND LISTENING

Listening to your mix at different volume levels is important, as only one level could fool you.

As you go further in mixing, remember to take breaks to just listen to your mix at different volume levels. These volume levels usually are: *barely audible, comfortable listening level* and *very loud*. They have different functions. When you set your listening level to barely audible, you will instantly hear which elements dominate the mix in volume, and in a good mix every important element should be audible at a very low level. With a normal listening level you should be able to have a discussion with your friends without the music taking over the sound space. Also, at this level you will hear the punchiness and the dynamics of your mix easily. Lastly, turning the volume very high to almost when it starts to hurt your ears is a handy listening method from time to time, revealing mix problems with instruments that are too loud and are uncomfortable to listen to compared to the rest of the audio. Bass is also smart to check at high volumes from time to time.

How to: Reference your mix at different levels and make mix changes

1. Listen at a very low level. Make sure you can hear every important element clearly even at a barely audible level. If something seems to "drown" in the mix, bring its mixer fader

up little by little until heard again. If something dominates the mix too much, turn it down a notch.

2. Listen at a comfortable "discussion" level. Listen to the dynamics and punchiness of your mix. Is something too loud or too quiet, fighting with the general dynamics of your mix? Again, adjust with the mixer fader to compensate.

3. Listen at a very loud level. Listen to instruments and elements that might actually "hurt" your ears a little bit while listening. If you can spot elements like this, bring them down with the fader a little bit until they sound more pleasant to you.

4. As you go further in the mixing process, repeat the level referencing from time to time and adjust fader levels accordingly.

Pro Tip: Listening at different levels is an important process, all of them bringing something to the table for optimal listening results in every possible environment, such as a car stereo, living room, computer desk speakers or a very loud club sound system. The point is to make music sound as good as it possibly can no matter what the playback system or volume level is.

Chapter 1 Mix Essentials

05 SPECTRUM ANALYZERS

Spectrum analyzers bring an extra eye to a mix and offer a visual representation of a mix.

While mixing is (and ultimately should be) done by ear, using a spectrum analyzer can greatly ease the process of mixing. The spectrum analyzer will show the frequency spread of your mix, reveal possible areas with either a lack or abundance of frequencies and give you hints whether you have achieved a nice mix balance. Free spectrum analyzer plugins can be found on the Internet, such as Voxengo SPAN. Many modern EQ plugins have a spectrum analyzer built in as well.

How to: Use the spectrum analyzer in various scenarios

1. Insert the spectrum analyzer plugin on your master bus so it will analyze the whole track.

2. B*alancing the low end and the high end*: how does the low end (40-200 Hz) compare to the high end (1-20 kHz) on the analyzer. Are they roughly at the same level or are they way off in level? For example: if the bass end is way below the high end in the spectrum analyzer, you could bring the high end elements down in the mix to compensate for a more balanced and pleasant-sounding mix.

3. *Finding loose peaks in the mix*: sometimes, sudden peaks can throw the mix balance a bit off and introduce too much

dynamics. The usual scenario would include an unprocessed vocal, which is very dynamic by its nature. Peaks are easily spotted in a spectrum analyzer by finding scattered, uneven "pillars" in frequency and volume. Further action can be taken either with the fader or a peak-taming compressor, if needed.

4. *Finding frequency "dips" in the mix*: if your mix is lacking certain frequencies, you can spot them as "holes" in the spectrum. This helps you to spot problematic areas and potentially fixing them by boosting frequencies in these areas with an EQ or adding new instruments for a fuller sounding mix.

Pro Tip #1: Never mix solely by looking at a spectrum analyzer, but take note of the visual hints given by it and try to listen accordingly. The spectrum analyzer shouldn't be trusted in every case, because if it sounds right, it is right. For example: if a spectrum analyzer reveals to you a series of dramatic peaks in the mix, you should try to pinpoint which sources of audio are causing those peaks and further determine whether the peaks are a good or bad thing. In the end, trust your ears. If you like how things sound, leave them alone.

Pro Tip #2: Insert spectrum analyzers on instrument group buses such as drums and music to look and analyze the frequencies in the specific instrument groups, getting a macro-level picture of the frequencies.

Chapter 1 Mix Essentials

CHAPTER 2 MIX CLARITY

06 GET RID OF UNWANTED FREQUENCIES

Getting rid of unneeded frequencies in instruments will dramatically clarify a mix.

After achieving a nice mix balance by using faders, clearing unwanted frequencies with an equalizer is the big number two. Essentially, EQ'ing your channels properly will already make a mix. The rest is just extra spice. Getting rid of unwanted frequencies is done by cutting frequencies with an equalizer. You can use your stock equalizer plugin in your DAW or a third-party EQ, but you will want to use a transparent and clean EQ for this task to stealthily remove bad frequencies from the audio.

How to: EQ your channels for a clean mix

1. Insert an EQ plugin on the channel you want. Any transparent digital EQ will do, such as the stock EQ in your DAW.

2. Listen first and try to determine if there are some frequency areas you don't like in the sound.

3. Boost a bell-shaped EQ band up to about 10dB and sweep the frequency around until you find the spot that sounds

bad. Then cut the frequency until the annoying or harsh sound disappears. The cut could be anywhere from -1 to -10dB.

3. Use the plugin bypass –function to your advantage to constantly compare the equalized signal to the original signal to find out whether you have successfully EQ'd the channel – or not. The bypass button is your friend.

4. Adjust the Q value to find the desired character for the cut. The Q of an EQ band means the bandwidth. Smaller Q values affect a larger area of frequencies and larger values affect a narrower area. A Q value of 1 would result in a wide cut, audibly affecting the tone of the sound, but a value of 10 would be more surgical and precise. Use your ears to set the final Q value.

Pro Tip #1: Instead of boosting and sweeping the EQ band to find bad frequencies from an audio signal, use cutting and sweeping. This method is a bit more advanced since you'll have to listen carefully which frequencies disappear while you sweep. This is the method I personally prefer because it never lies: if the dirt disappears and the sound becomes clearer and more pleasant, you have found the problem frequency.

Pro Tip #2: Always EQ with the entire song playing, because that allows you to hear the EQ changes in the context of the music. Solo EQ'ing is not recommended except if you need to pinpoint a problematic frequency. Always check your EQ changes in the context of a mix.

Chapter 2 Mix Clarity

07 COMPLEMENTARY EQ

Complementary EQ will fix issues with two or more elements "fighting" for the same frequency space.

First and foremost, true complementary equalization is already done in the arrangement stage, simply making two similar elements not fight for the same space. But in reality, this is often not possible all the time, therefore bringing the EQ to the rescue. The concept of complementary EQ revolves around determining important frequency areas in signals and making room for those important areas with an EQ by reducing those same frequencies in other signals.

How to: EQ a lead vocal and an electric guitar in a complementary way

1. Insert an EQ to both channels and bring both plugins on top to the screen.

2. Determine important or good sounding frequency areas for both elements by boosting and sweeping the EQ around. Leave a mark to those frequencies by bypassing the EQ bands.

3. If the vocal's important frequency would be at 2000 Hz, you would apply a cut in the guitar's EQ at 2000 Hz. This way, you will free space for the vocal which has its crucial frequency at 2000 Hz. Try 1-3dB cuts and don't go too far, so the tonal balance of the instruments won't be affected too much.

4. Repeat the complementary EQ technique for major and important elements in the mix to further clarify them.

Pro Tip #1: Use complementary EQ'ing in instrument group buses. For example: If all the music instruments are dominating the 500 Hz area, you could apply a small cut to all the drums and basses in that frequency.

Pro Tip #2: You can apply a small boost to important frequencies, and cut the same frequencies by the same amount in other instruments. If you boost a vocal 2dB at 4000 Hz, you would cut the electric guitar by -2dB at 4000 Hz.

08 EQ the Send Effects

Be sure to equalize the aux channels where your send effects are, such as reverbs or delays.

The usual scenario is this: you put a reverb on a channel where you send different instruments to in order to get a nice unifying reverb sound. But then you forget to EQ that reverb channel, because you don't see it as an instrument. It is important to EQ send effect channels because they will quickly clog up your mix if not done so. The reason why they clog the mix is because the instruments that are sent to the effected channels become blurred by the inserted effect and therefore lose some clarity. Send effects should enhance the original sounds, not get in their way. Always remember to EQ your send effects properly for a professional sounding mix. Think of them as just another instrument channel.

How to: EQ a reverb send channel

1. Create an auxiliary track (or bus track), insert a reverb on it as 100% wet and send an instrument signal to that reverb aux by using the sends in your DAW.

2. Insert an EQ plugin on the aux channel.

3. Create a high pass filter on the EQ first to cut unwanted low end frequencies. Set the high pass filter to around 200-700

Hz, depending on how much low end you want to preserve in the reverb.

4. Create a normal bell-shaped EQ band and boost while doing a frequency sweep (or cut and sweep) to find the frequencies that mask the original sound too much.

5. Create an EQ cut with the band, cutting as much as needed to clarify the signal. Use Q values of 1 to 4 for a wide, tone-shaping cut.

6. Create more bands and cut more if needed until the reverb sounds great and complements the original sound.

Pro Tip: You should at least insert a high pass filter on every send effect channel to clean up the low end. Sometimes it's alright to let the effects "take over", if you actually like to drown your instruments in reverb or delay for example.

09 SIDE CHAIN COMPRESSION

Side chain compression is one of the secret tools in a mixer's toolbox to make a clear, punchy mix.

Everyone knows the classic pumping effect of a kick and bass in dance music, which is a prime and somewhat radical example of side chain compression. In that case, the kick drum's audio signal is essentially sent to the compressor's side chain input on the bass channel, so the compressor is triggered by the kick drum, causing gain reduction on the bass whenever the kick hits. Taking this popular method further, side chain compression is a great all around mixing trick which will introduce tons of clarity and punch in your mixes. Side chain compression is also a highly creative mixing trick. In the following example we'll look at using side chain compression subtly to create focus for a bassline, which needs to be up front and out of everything else's way.

How to: Create focus for a giant bassline by compressing elements playing simultaneously

1. Insert a compressor with a side chain function to each channel you want out of the bassline's way, such as a busy hi-hat line or a sustaining synth pad.

2. Set the bassline as the side chain input to trigger the compressor. Look into your DAW's manual for more information on how to enable side chaining.

3. For starters, use medium attack and medium release for the compressor (30ms attack, 60ms release).

4. Turn down the threshold until you get lots (down to -20dB) of gain reduction in the compressor.

5. Adjust the attack and release to react musically to the side chain signal (see tip #21).

6. Back up the threshold until you get 1-3dB of gain reduction in the compressor for a subtle but effective ducking effect.

7. Remember, this is a subtle mixing trick to gently bring elements into focus in a mix, while the elements that are being compressed will still be clearly audible in the mix. The point here is not to cause dance music –like pumping. The compressor's duty should be merely to give some room for the elements in need of focus.

Pro Tip #1: Think of side chain compression as a technique to use whenever you need an element to have focus in the mix, making other instruments duck in volume automatically.

Pro Tip #2: Go wild with the gain reduction in a side chain compressor as you could get a very cool effect by doing so. In the end, use your ears to tune the compressor's threshold value together with the attack and release. Using side chain compressors creatively is a ton of fun.

Chapter 2 Mix Clarity

10 CLEAN YOUR AUDIO TRACKS

By making sure all your audio is clean and free of artifacts, you are one step closer to a tight, professional sound.

The process of audio editing is a demanding but necessary step in all audio and music production. Mainly by creating fades and cutting out unnecessary audio information the tracks will have so much more clarity. As mixers and music producers, our responsibility is to keep our sound at high standards and include only the audio information that is needed. Make sure to clean up your audio tracks because they will positively affect the entirety of a song.

How to: Clean up a vocal track using fades and cutting audio

1. Create a quick fade-in right before the vocal becomes audible, to remove all unnecessary microphone bleed and other nasty artifacts or noise. By creating fades you will get rid of sudden clicks and pops as well. Create a fade-out in the end. You can do this either with a DAW's fade function or by automating the volume of audio tracks.

2. Hidden artifacts, clicks and pops might lie in between of sung lines and phrases. Cut them out from the audio and create fades for the remaining edges of audio which are left from the cut.

3. If wanted, cut excessive breath sounds from the tracks.

Pro Tip #1: Insert an EQ with a high pass filter to tracks where the subsonic frequency information is not needed, such as in a vocal track. In a vocal track, setting a high pass filter to 100 Hz will noticeably clean up the track, getting rid of the low-end rumble while keeping the vocal focused. Ideally, you want to insert a high pass filter to every track in your mix, except for crucial elements such as the kick drum or sub bass, where the low end is needed.

Pro Tip #2: Take advantage of noise gates. By using a gate, you can automate the process of removing low-level clicks, pops, artifacts and noise from an audio track, such as from the pauses of a vocal track. Use the threshold of the gate to set the level below which sound becomes muted.

Chapter 2 Mix Clarity

Chapter 3 Drum Sweetening

11 Tuned Kick Drum

A great kick drum is the foundation of every piece of electronic music. Tune it for the biggest musical impact in the low frequencies.

The tuning of a kick drum is important especially because of the low end frequencies it has. If these frequencies were fighting with the musicality of the rest of the song, the whole song's musical presentation could be compromised. By tuning kick drums, you will assure a solid bottom foundation for your music, which will have a huge impact on the total punch and musicality of your tracks. The important thing is to tune the kick drum according to the musical rules of your song. For example: if your track is written in G minor, a safe bet is to tune the kick to the note of G, which is the root note in the G minor chord, as well as the tonic note in the scale of G minor. You can also tune the kick drum to any note that belongs to the scale. Trust me on this. You will want to tune your kick drums.

How to: Tune a kick drum by pitch shifting and using a spectrum analyzer for help

1. Let's assume you have your kick drum loaded into a sampler where you are triggering it from.

2. Insert a spectrum analyzer on the kick drum channel so you can see the low end peak. *Note*: this low end bump of the kick drum will dictate the exact tuning of the kick drum.

3. Start pitch shifting the kick by using your sampler's pitch function. While you do this, look at the spectrum analyzer and you'll see the kick drum's low end peak move to the direction you pitch shift it to.

4. When you have arrived in the ballpark of the right pitch for the kick, zoom in on the spectrum analyzer to fine-tune the tuning of the kick.

Pro Tip #1: Pitch shift the kick drum two octaves up before tuning it, this way you can clearly hear the tone of the kick and find the exact note value for it when tuning it.

Pro Tip #2: Play a simple sine wave note from a synthesizer for the note you want to tune the kick into. This will act as a tuner to match the kick drum's tone to, just like a guitarist tuning his guitar into a piano note.

Pro Tip #3: Use frequency values and their responding musical notes to your advantage in tuning. For example, 55 Hz equals to the note of A. You'll find a list by MTU Physics at the following link:

http://www.phy.mtu.edu/~suits/notefreqs.html

Chapter 3 Drum Sweetening

12 Fat Kick Drum

Fat, punchy, deep – these adjectives are desirable for a kick drum. You can have one too.

Great kick drums always go back to a great source sound. While the original kick sound is the most important part, a lot can be achieved with a simple EQ and some saturation to further adjust the tone of the kick drum. By using the EQ to shave off the mud from the kick, you will make the kick drum breathe in the low end and have that punchy midrange depth all professional records seem to have in their kicks. To finalize the tone of a fat kick drum, a tape machine emulation or saturation plugin is your friend. Try the free Saturation Knob by Softube.

How to: EQ the kick drum for fatness and apply some tape saturation

1. Insert your favorite EQ plugin to your kick drum track.

2. Create wide EQ cuts in the ranges of 200-400 Hz and 500-1000 Hz. Leave the Q value to 1-4 for a wide cut. Try 2-5dB cuts first, but cut down to -8dB if needed.

3. Create EQ boosts around the dominant sub frequencies (45-55 Hz) and the bass frequencies (80-100 Hz). Boost up to 3dB or more if needed. Set the Q for a tighter value for the boosts, around 3-8.

4. If you need more punch, try boosting the frequencies in the area of 100-150 Hz with a wider Q value (1.5-3). To emphasize the click of the kick drum, try boosting above 4000 Hz.

5. Insert a tape emulation or saturation plugin after the EQ.

6. Drive the signal into the tape machine or saturator so the kick drum starts to have noticeable punch and extra harmonic content.

7. If one exists, use the tape emulation's or saturator's dry/wet control to tone down the effect a bit. Around 50% of tape processing is good for keeping the original punch of the kick.

Pro Tip #1: While cutting frequencies with an EQ, listen with focus and aim to cut those areas that seem to improve the low end punch and depth of the kick drum. Listen carefully to the low end and how it opens up while EQ'ing. Bypass the EQ regularly to hear the before and after effect for objective results.

Pro Tip #2: Apply a filter as a last step in the plugin chain to shave off some of the digital highs. The kick will actually get noticeably deeper because the low and mid-punch frequencies get the spotlight.

Chapter 3 Drum Sweetening

13 HUGE CLAP AND SNARE

The key to a huge big room clap or snare lies in its effects.

When you want to create a larger-than-life snare, you need to understand what it is that makes it so big. It all comes down to the room sound – a reverb plugin. In order to create a huge clap, you need to create an aux track where you'll insert the reverb. Here's the crucial part: totally smash the reverb with a very fast compressor to get a huge, aggressive sound. Then you can use the reverb channel's mixer fader to feed in the volume of the reverb, adjusting the total "room" size of the snare or clap.

How to: Create a huge clap using reverb

1. Create an aux track where you can send the clap's signal and insert a reverb on it, 100% wet.

2. Find a relatively short, room type reverb sound, around 1-2 seconds of length.

3. Insert a compressor on the reverb channel using very fast compression settings. Start with the fastest attack and release to completely smash the sound. Use a very high ratio (20:1).

4. Aim for plenty of gain reduction for a rough, smashing sound (-10 to -15dB or more).

5. Mix the reverb to taste, complementing the dry clap sound.

Pro Tip #1: When you send the clap to the aux channel using a send, make it a pre-fader send, meaning that the original clap's fader position doesn't affect the volume of the send – it sends the signal to the aux before the fader.

Pro Tip #2: Route your clap and compressed reverb to an aux and compress them together for even a bigger impact.

Chapter 3 Drum Sweetening

14 LARGE GATED PERCUSSION

By smart use of gates and reverb, your percussion will become huge but retain lots of punchiness.

The idea of using reverb to create large percussion sounds is done in mixing studios every day. The real secret is to use a gate with a side chain trigger to switch the reverb on and off. Your percussion sound will dictate the opening and closing of the gate on the reverb, creating a huge but tight sound in total. In other words, whenever your percussion sound is audible, so is the reverb, but when the percussion stops playing, the reverb is cut as well, not providing an unneeded reverb tail.

How to: Use reverb and a gate to create large but tight percussion

1. Create an aux track and insert a reverb on it, 100% wet. Send the percussion signal to it.

2. Insert a gate with a side chain function on the aux track after the reverb. Set the side chain input as the percussion signal.

3. Adjust the threshold so the gate opens when the percussion hits and closes when it is inaudible.

4. Fine-tune the attack and release to smoothen the curve of the noise gate and adjust the length of the reverb.

Pro Tip #1: Need a longer reverb tail? Create another reverb aux track to send the percussion into. The extra reverb will bring a reverb tail, for even a more massive feel. Don't gate this reverb though for the effect to work.

Pro Tip #2: See tip #13 for compressing the reverb. Try to compress your reverb before you apply the gate for intensity.

Chapter 3 Drum Sweetening

15 PARALLEL COMPRESSION PUNCH

Any pro mixer's secret weapon: parallel compression.

Parallel compression is a technique where the original signal is routed to an auxiliary track, and the aux track is being compressed while the original signal remains dry. Thus, the aux track can be mixed in with the original signal to create a meatier and punchier entity. Parallel compression is a favorite especially on drums, but works great on any dynamic source in need of compression, such as vocals. The point of parallel compression is to retain the dynamics and brilliance of the original source without smashing it with compression, letting the parallel compressor do it instead, either subtly or aggressively.

How to: Improve punch by focusing on the transients of drums using parallel compression

1. Create an aux track and send all your drums to it. Make it a pre-fader send so the sent signal remains static and isn't affected by the original volume fader positions of the drums.

2. Insert a compressor on the aux track.

3. Compress the signal to get a large amount of gain reduction, down to -10 to -20dB.

4. Set a large ratio, such as 20:1.

5. Set the attack to fast to hear some smack on the transients, but keep the release medium. Good starting points are a 15ms attack and 300ms release.

6. Set a faster release for snappiness and intensity, if wanted.

7. Control the impact of the parallel compression by adjusting the fader of the parallel aux.

Pro Tip #1: Find the sweet spot of the parallel punch. Setting the parallel aux's fader midway is a great starting point in finding the sweet spot, where the punch is. If you feed too much of the parallel processed signal, you'll get an over-compressed sound, which beats the point of parallel compression.

Pro Tip #2: Try different compressors for parallel compression. Ideally, you'd want to try some character compressors for the task, especially the emulations of classic hardware, for a really nice vibe.

Chapter 3 Drum Sweetening

Chapter 4 Special Stereo Width

16 Micro Pitch Shifters

The micro pitch shifter is a classic stereo widening trick.

Micro pitch shifting is an old stereo widening technique, involving a quick stereo delay with pitch shifting each side (left and right) to the opposite directions (up and down). The micro shifting trick is especially useful for melodic instruments and vocals, making them extremely wide in the stereo image while gaining a pleasant detuned character. There are various plugins out there to get the job done, but the effect can be achieved by doing it by hand as well, which is what we are doing here right now.

How to: Create a custom, simple micro pitch shift effect

1. Take a mono source and duplicate it on a new track. Pan the original one 100% left and the duplicate 100% right.

2. Nudge (move) the duplicate to the right a few milliseconds (5-20ms) so it is slightly delayed compared to the original one.

3. Tune down the original audio a few cents (1-20 cents) by using a pitch shifting plugin, such as the stock pitch shifter in your DAW. Tune up the duplicate by a similar amount.

4. Play back to hear the pitch shift effect and the wider stereo image.

5. Fine tune the nudge (delay) and detune values to taste.

Pro Tip #1: The bigger the delay between the two signals, the wider the sound will be.

Pro Tip #2: When setting the detune values, don't set the exact same values to get some natural difference in pitch and therefore a more natural sound.

17 HAAS EFFECT

The Haas effect is a classic delay effect, creating a super wide stereo sound.

When something needs to be extra wide, the Haas effect is the way to go. It's great to use on drum hits, backing vocals, sound effects or anything that simply needs to be wide in the stereo field. The Haas effect is based on a small delay between the left and right channels in a signal. It is easily done with any stereo delay plugin.

How to: Use a stereo delay to widen your hats creating the Haas effect

1. Insert a stereo delay on your hi-hat channel. Make the delay 100% wet.

2. Use a dual echo delay -mode where you can customize the delay time in milliseconds for both left and right channels individually.

3. For the left channel, set the delay amount to 0 ms. For the right channel, make the delay amount to anything between 7-21 ms. Play back to hear the effect.

4. Fine tune the value in milliseconds to control the desired width of the effect and the delay between the channels.

35

Pro Tip: Go overboard with the millisecond settings to create a wide stereo slapback effect. Try a setting of 60-90 ms for best results. Try this on melodic, sustained instruments, such as a piano for a beautiful stereo impact.

Chapter 4 Special Stereo Width

18 Panning Mono Reverbs

Panning mono reverbs will support a wide and clear stereo image.

Panning a mono reverb is an unpopular method, since most plugin reverbs are stereo reverbs. However, panning mono reverbs around the stereo field can make a more focused mix and an excellent effect when certain instruments are concerned. The focus happens because the reverb isn't allowed to take over the whole stereo field. Remember, you have to make both the source sound and the reverb mono for this trick to work properly.

How to: Create a stereo image panning a mono source and mono reverb to the opposite directions

1. Let's assume you have a guitar sound, which is recorded in mono. Send the guitar to a new mono aux track.

2. Insert a mono reverb on the aux track. Set the reverb 100% wet.

3. Pan the original guitar track 100% to the left and the reverb aux 100% to the right.

4. You will now have a nice stereo image, with the dry signal on the left and the wet reverbed signal on the right.

Pro Tip #1: If your DAW doesn't support mono tracks or if you don't have a mono reverb, you can use a free tool such as bx solo by Brainworx to force your stereo signal into mono, and then pan it around the sound field.

Pro Tip #2: Get creative with panning mono reverbs. Let's say your guitar is panned 50% to the left. Try panning its mono reverb 100% to the left, for an interesting effect. You could also pan the reverb right where the original sound is, in this case 50% to the left, to support the original sound and pinpoint its location in the mix.

19 RHYTHMIC STEREO DELAYS

Delays are the oldest (and coolest) trick in the mixer's toolbox, and very stylish when used rhythmically.

Rhythmic delays equals musical results. They can enhance a performance to great heights by supporting the rhythm already in the performance. In this sense, delays could be used to divide the rhythm into smaller increments or to create a rhythmic tail for longer, sustained hits. For example, if a piano groove is played in quarter notes (1/4), a delay could be used to bring out the eight notes (1/8) to support the performance for a more moving feel. Or, if the same piano would play long stabs in whole notes (1/1), a delay could be used to create a rhythmic tail in quarter notes to create continuity. In stereo, rhythmic delay effects work especially well as a ping-pong delay, going from one side to another, or just as a stereo echo. *Note*: the delay needs to have a tempo synchronization – function to lock the tempo of your song to the delay. Luckily, almost all modern delays have this function.

How to: Create a rhythmic delay using any delay plugin of choice

1. Insert the delay on a rhythmic instrument, such as a piano or guitar.

2. Enable the tempo synchronization –function on the delay, to lock the delay to the correct tempo.

3. Choose the delay time to suit your material (half, quarter, eight, sixteenth notes).

4. Try different delay modes: ping-pong, stereo echo or dual-mono echo mode. Choose which mode you like the best by listening.

5. Have fun with rhythmic delays and create interesting rhythmic patterns!

Pro Tip: With a delay plugin such as <u>Soundtoys Echoboy</u>, you'll be able to control the groove of the delay, meaning the amount of shuffle or swing, which will enhance the feel of the delay even more. Note that EchoBoy is not a free plugin.

Chapter 4 Special Stereo Width

20 AUTOMATIC PANNERS

Panning doesn't necessarily have to be static by using only pan knobs – let the machine do it for you to create interesting motion.

Automatic panners are the easiest tools to use in order to create stereo movement in a song. Autopan effects bring a song to life with zero effort. You could easily autopan key elements of a mix to make them stand out from the ones that remain static. Autopanners work best on mono sources, but you could also easily apply them to stereo sources to make them move in the sound field. Autopanners are also called tremolo plugins. Most DAWs have them by default. Great commercial autopanners are <u>Panstation by Audio Damage</u> and <u>PanMan by Soundtoys</u>.

How to: Create a rhythmic autopan effect to an instrument

1. Insert an autopan plugin on your instrument track.

2. Switch on the tempo synchronization on the plugin.

3. Adjust the rhythm (or speed) of the autopan to taste by using note values.

4. Use the depth –function on the plugin to control the mix of the autopan effect versus the original source. This is also called a "mix" or "wet/dry" knob.

Pro Tip #1: Use autopanners in "free" –mode so they are not locked to tempo and adjust the panning rate manually. This will give a more natural feeling to a song with the panning motion moving freely in the stereo field.

Pro Tip #2: Make the autopan effect very narrow, barely widening the original source to result in a subtle but consciously noticeable effect that brings life and movement to a mix.

CHAPTER 5 ADVANCED MIXING TECHNIQUES

21 MUSICAL SIDE CHAIN COMPRESSION

Everyone can accomplish the pumping side chain compression effect typical to dance music, but only a few achieve truly musical results from it.

The key to groovy side chain compression is in the tuning of the threshold, attack and release values. The goal here is to fine tune any side chain compression effect to the song at hand, because all music is different and behave differently. While the attack function plays an important role by shaping the initial transient, the release is the function that can make or break a side chain compression effect. The following is a proven method of getting your side chain compression curves musical and tight.

How to: Create a musical, pumping side chain compression effect on a sustaining pad sound with a kick drum

1. Insert a compressor on the pad channel and enable side chaining on it.

2. Select the kick drum as the source of the side chain, so the compressor starts working whenever the kick drum hits.

3. Set both attack and release to the fastest. Set a ratio of 3:1 and pull down the threshold to get about -20dB of gain reduction.

4. Start bringing up the release slowly until you find a sweet spot where the compression pumps tightly to the beat and isn't too fast or too slow.

5. Start bringing up the attack to find a sweet spot for the transient, so it isn't crushed totally by the compressor. Adjust to taste.

6. When you have found musical attack and release settings, adjust the threshold again to find an optimal balance of gain reduction. This is a matter of taste, but the range between -6 to -20dB is a good starting point to find a punchy side chain groove.

Pro Tip #1: Have a basic house hi-hat groove (eight notes) play while you adjust the side chain compression. The trick is to listen to the hi-hats hit and adjust the release of the side chain so it is in time with the hi-hat hitting. In other words, make the compression return back to normal just before or right when the hi-hat hits, for musical results.

Pro Tip #2: Apply a very small amount of side chain compression to your drums to barely shave off the transients a bit for a tighter, subtly compressed feel. This method could tighten up claps, snares, hats and the rest of your drums. The range of -1 to -3dB should offer enough gain reduction without crushing your drums.

Chapter 5 Advanced Mixing Techniques

22 AUTOMATING FADER LEVELS

Fader level automation is an advanced mixing technique and most often than not, essential.

Mixes don't necessarily remain intact through the whole way of the song, because at some parts certain instruments and elements might be too quiet or too loud compared to other parts in the song. This is why fader level automation is a simple technique to remedy these issues, but rarely used by beginners in mixing. A great example is a vocal track. The verse sounds good in the mix, just at the right level, but when the chorus arrives, the vocal drowns into the mix because of other additive instruments. The cure to this? Bring up the fader level of the vocal for only the chorus parts, to bring it forward again in the mix. Level fader automation can be done on any instrument that demands it.

How to: Automate the fader to boost vocal levels for a chorus

1. Enable volume automation for the vocal channel. Find out how this is done in your DAW by referring to the user guide or manual. You should be able to see a volume automation line which can be further automated by clicking to add nodes and modifying them.

2. Create one node in the beginning of the volume boost and one where you want the boost to return to normal.

3. Boost the area by 1-3dB to bring out the vocal. This is usually done by dragging the line between the two nodes upwards.

4. Make sure the boost returns back to normal level in the end.

5. Repeat the process for any parts in need of volume boosts (or cuts!)

Pro Tip #1: Aside from fader level automation, you could use audio specific gain to turn up certain parts, if you have a clip gain or audio gain function in your DAW. Make note though, that by using clip gain, the volume of the audio will be turned up before it hits your mixer channel – before the fader and any processing you might have. Essentially, you are turning up the input gain of the audio this way, which is another handy method for gain staging (see tip #01).

Pro Tip #2: Use fader automation to create climaxes. For example, before a drop, you could automate certain elements to rise in volume to create a climatic and energetic rise, implying that something bigger is going to happen next.

Pro Tip #3: Try detailed volume automation to bring up only certain words in a vocal, chords or melody pieces in instruments. Very often, volume level automation will remedy issues in a cleaner manner that would otherwise lead to the use of compression.

23 FILTER AUTOMATION

Filter automation is a recognizable and "famous" element in electronic music.

Everyone has heard of wobble basses and rising noise sweeps in electronic music. They are done with filter automation. A filter is essentially a one band EQ – usually a low pass filter when it comes to filter automation. This means the filter will cut off high frequencies at the specified frequency point. The fun thing is, this point can be automated within your DAW to create interesting sounds by shifting the filter around the frequency spectrum.

How to: Create a rising white noise sweep by using a noise synthesizer and a filter

1. Open your synthesizer of choice and play a simple white noise from it. All modern synthesizer plugins should have a white noise oscillator.

2. Insert a filter on the synth channel and enable automation for the frequency. Again, refer to your DAW's manual to find out how to enable plugin parameter automation.

3. Create two nodes in the automation line – one in the beginning and one in the end where you want the filter automation to stop.

4. Make the first node 400 Hz and the end node 18 kHz. You should have a nice and smooth rising line in the automation lane. Play it back to hear the sweeping effect.

5. Use the peak (also known as resonance or Q) function on the filter to change the tone of the sweep, bringing out some nice resonances to sweeten the effect.

Pro Tip #1: If you don't have a filter plugin, you can use the stock EQ plugin in your DAW. You just need to create a low pass filter (or high cut) and automate it to act as a filter.

Pro Tip #2: To create wobbling effects, enable the modulation in your filter to make the filter move automatically. Synchronize the filter to the tempo of your song for musical results and choose the desired note value for the rhythm.

Chapter 5 Advanced Mixing Techniques

24 Creating Reverb and Delay Tails

Reverbs and delays not only work well as static elements in a mix, but as special spice and glue.

Reverb and delay tails are useful for gluing parts of a song together, such as a verse and a chorus. You would make the reverb and delay tails just like creating regular reverb and delay effects, but you would automate their volume in and out at specific parts of a song. In a sense, they would work as special effects that would surprise the listener and create extra value for the track.

How to: Bridge song parts together by creating special reverb and delay tails

1. Create a reverb or delay aux and send the original signal there as you would when creating a normal reverb or delay aux track send. Set the effect 100% wet.

2. You need to enable automation for the send level to the aux and not the volume automation of the auxiliary track itself (*important!*)

3. With the send level automation line, bring it all the way down for the whole duration of the song, so nothing is sent to the effects.

4. Create rises in the sections you choose to send signal into the reverb or delay to create momentary special effects. Click on the automation line to add nodes and create volume boosts to let the send actually *send* some signal into the effects. Refer to Tip #22 if you are having problems with the automation line.

Pro Tip #1: Create rhythmic delay tails to highlight certain words in a vocal track, for a cool effect. Try quarter and eight note delays for this.

Pro Tip #2: Go wild with the reverb decay time and the delay feedback times — you could create an endless wash of reverb or a long echo of delay by doing so.

Chapter 5 Advanced Mixing Techniques

25 AUTOMATING PLUGIN PARAMETERS

Dig deeper into your plugins and automate their parameters to bring things into life in your mixes and music.

By automating different parameters of your plugins and instruments, you will learn a lot how different sounds are made. A fine example of plugin parameter automation is to automate the attack, decay, sustain and release envelopes, or ADSR, in your synthesizers or samplers. Since the ADSR envelope is a vital element to any synthesizer sound, why not automate it for a deeper effect? The lesson to learn from this is, you can automate nearly every parameter of any plugin, with only your creativity as the limit. The quality of your productions and mixes will greatly improve with the use of parameter automation.

How to: Automate a synthesizer ADSR envelope for variety in sound

1. Create your synthesizer sound and create a rhythmic, fast-paced pattern with eight notes.

2. Enable automation for the attack and decay of the ADSR envelope to control the transient sound and the volume decay of the synth.

3. While your synthesizer pattern is playing, automate the attack from its original position to a slower attack, to create a sweeping effect for the synth's attack.

4. Similarly to the attack, automate the decay at parts of your synth pattern to further diversify the sound, creating a shorter pop or a longer, decaying stab sound.

Pro Tip #1: Use ADSR automation in combination with filter automation of the synthesizer for even a more professional touch.

Pro Tip #2: Experiment with plugin parameter automation! Music doesn't need to be static, so introduce some variety to it. Try to automate various parameters in your effects plugins, filters, synthesizers, distortion or any type of plugin you can think of.

HEY, I HOPE YOU ENJOYED THIS BOOK. CHECK OUT MY OTHER BOOKS TO SUPPORT YOU IN MAKING MUSIC AND STAY ON TOP OF YOUR MUSIC PRODUCTION GAME...

-Roy Wilkenfeld

Making Music: 25 Motivational Creativity Tips for Electronic Music Production

Music Theory: Simple Music Theory for Electronic Music Production: Beginner's Guide to Rhythm, Chords, Scales, Modes and a lot, lot more...

THANK YOU FOR READING THIS BOOK

Please check out the Production Wisdom blog for more great tips and information about mixing, music production, techniques and philosophy.

productionwisdom.com

Made in the USA
Monee, IL
22 December 2019

19439083R00035